The Worlds
of
King Lear

Darlene Mathis Eddy

BALL STATE MONOGRAPH NUMBER TWENTY

ℭ𝔥e 𝔖i𝔯t𝔥 𝔅ooke. 𝔉o.𝔠𝔯liii.

Frontispiece   The Figure of Fortune in John Lydgate's *The Fall of Princes* (London, 1554).

> For thee, oppressèd King, am I cast down.
> Myself could else outfrown false fortune's frown.   (*King Lear*, V. iii. 5-6)

Reprinted from Samuel Claggett Chew, *The Pilgrimage of Life* (New Haven, 1962) by permission of Yale University Press.

The Worlds of *King Lear*

Darlene Mathis Eddy

Associate Professor of English
Ball State University

BALL STATE MONOGRAPH NUMBER TWENTY
Publications in English, No. 14
Ball State University, Muncie, Indiana 47306
1970

For
the memory of my mother
Fern Roose Paulmer Mathis
and
for my father
William Eugene Mathis

"And summer's lease hath all too short a date."

Acknowledgments

The critical spirit and aesthetic perspectives of many whose efforts have made possible the detailed investigation of that art which "was not of an age, but for all time" have provided a rich heritage from which this paper draws. Readers conversant with major Shakespearean studies will recognize my indebtedness to Samuel Taylor Coleridge, Andrew Cecil Bradley, Arthur Sewell, Theodore Spencer, Robert Heilman, Alfred Harbage, and Maynard Mack. I remain especially grateful to Francis Fergusson for setting an example of disciplined scholarship and humanistic commitment that makes possible the meaningful exploration of literature.

To Richard W. Burkhardt, Vice President for Instructional Affairs and Dean of Faculties, and to the Ball State University Faculty Research Grant Program, I am grateful for encouragement and support.

To give thanks to colleagues at Ball State University is a pleasure. Frances Mayhew Rippy, Professor of English, generously gave of her time and critical insight in considering the material for publication. Alexander MacGibbon, Professor of English and Director of the Honors Program, evidenced gracious interest in the project. Daryl Adrian, current chairman of the Faculty Publications Committee, read the manuscript with responsive judgment as did the other members of the Committee: Ruth Myers, Helen Cloyd, Alice Hoover, Gertrude Kane, and Betty Memmott.

To thank the publishers who have kindly granted me permission to cite from various works is a privilege. All citations from *King Lear* are from the text included in *Shakespeare The Complete Works,* edited by G. B. Harrison (New York, 1968), and are reprinted by permission of Harcourt, Brace & World, Inc. The quotation from "Oration on the Dignity of Man" by Giovanni Pico Della Mirandola, translated by Elizabeth Livermore Forbes, is taken from *The Renaissance Philosophy of Man,* edited by Ernst Cassirer, Paul Oskar Kristeller, and John Herman Randall, Jr. (Chicago, 1948) (© 1948 by The University of Chicago) and is reprinted by permission of The University of Chicago Press. Quotations from *King Lear in Our Time* (Berkeley, 1965) by Maynard Mack are reprinted by permission of The Regents of the University of California. Quotations from *The Vision of Tragedy* (New Haven, 1959; reissued, 1962) by Richard Sewall are reprinted by permission of Yale University Press. Quotations from

"The World of the Traditional Monarchy" and "Introduction to *King Lear*" by Francis Fergusson are reprinted from *Shakespeare's Tragedies of Monarchy* (New York, 1958; reissued, 1962) by permission of Dell Publishing Company, Inc. Quotations from *Shakespeare and the Nature of Man* (New York, 1942; reissued, 1961) (© 1942, 1949, by The Macmillan Company) by Theodore Spencer are reprinted by permission of the Macmillan Company. Quotations from *Shakespearean Tragedy* (London, 1904; reprinted, New York, 1967) by Andrew Cecil Bradley are reprinted by permission of Macmillan & Co., Ltd., and St. Martin's Press, Inc.

The illustrations accompanying this study have been chosen from *The Pilgrimage of Life* (New Haven, 1962) by Samuel Claggett Chew and *Shakespeare and the Emblem Writers* (London, 1870; reprinted New York, 1966) by Henry Green. I am grateful to Yale University Press and to Burt Franklin for allowing me to reproduce the figures used in the Frontispiece and in Plates 1, 2, and 3. These illustrations are drawn from Renaissance materials which embody in emblem and iconography major concepts of the period. Their subjects are visual representations which impinge upon the controlling thematic and figurative patterns in the multi-dimensional worlds of *King Lear*: Fortune and her wheel, the cycle of life, the procession of the seasons, and the theatre of human life in which all men play their designated roles. Studied in relation to selected quotations from the tragedy, the illustrations add, perhaps, a vivid reinforcement to that dominant trope of the drama which emphasizes the temporal limitation of all human endeavor.

In the preparation of the manuscript, Dianne Guidone performed helpful services with sensitivity, and Elizabeth Martin made available her skills in photoduplication of materials.

To the students in English 465 and in Humanities 201-202-203 I express thanks for demonstrating the awareness that has allowed us to explore together areas of value and areas of artistry in the dramas of William Shakespeare.

To my most astute critic, Spencer L. Eddy, Jr., belong thanks for wit, patience, and a never-failing interest in things Shakespearean.

D.M.E.

Illustrations

The Worlds of *King Lear*

A London playgoer in 1607 might have jostled his way through the narrow streets of the city and crossed the Thames to Southwark to the Globe Theatre. While he waited to drop his penny into the admission box and enter the octagonal building with its tri-level stage and open roof, he might have mingled with a diverse group of people: a handful of noisy gallants, a baker, a shopowner and his wife, a trinket peddler, some noblemen, a few students from the Inns of Court, a band of apprentices, some craftsmen and laborers, a few clerks, some soldiers, and perhaps a pickpocket and a prostitute or two—in short, "a cross section of the London population"[1] for whom William Shakespeare wrote. While the crowd milled around the theatre, a balladeer might well have sung to them an old and well-known story:

> King Lear once rulèd in this land,
> With princely power and peace,
> And had all things with heart's content,
> That might his joys increase.[2]

From the simple tale in historical chronicles of the proud king of pagan Britain, Shakespeare was to create his greatest tragedy. Using the threads of fable and legend—the foolish monarch, the rash love test, the virtuous youngest daughter, the evil elder sisters—the drama weaves an intricate pattern around the nature of good and evil, the force of the destructive and creative spirit, the problems of kingship and power, and the question of justice and social equity. Within the narrative confines of the tale of Lear and his three daughters and the sub-plot of the Earl of Gloucester and his sons, an episode drawn from a minor incident in Sir Philip Sidney's *Arcadia*,[3] Shakespeare presents a multi-faceted world of human experience: king and subjects, husbands and wives, parents and children, servants and masters, brothers and sisters, lovers and friends. These relationships, moreover, are seen both in their ideal forms—what the dramatist terms "the offices of nature, bond of childhood,/Effects of courtesy, dues of gratitude"[4]—and in a state of chaotic and monstrous horror when those political, natural, and moral commitments which give order to life become inverted, weakened, or disrupted. It is a critical commonplace that *King Lear* contains many worlds.[5] The purpose of this study is to examine more closely four particular realms: the world

1

of metaphor, the world of action, the world of question, and the world of the humanistic vision.

Poets who speak with relevance and immediacy, as Aristotle noted some centuries ago, invariably have the gift of seeing resemblances in all aspects of existence. As he once wrote, ". . . by far the greatest thing for a poet is to be a master of metaphor. . . . It is a mark of genius, for to be good at metaphor is to be intuitively aware of hidden resemblances."[6] The metaphorical texture of *King Lear* maintains a richness and vastness that fuses the cosmological elements of earth, air, fire, and water with the most specific and particular observations of human conduct. Shakespearean scholars have commented at length on the frequent references in the play to violent weather, birds and beasts of prey, torture and wounds, extreme states of darkness and light, disease and infection, and acts of horror.[7] These patterns relate, of course, to basic motivations in character and action, to major themes, and to central moral issues. One possible way of approaching the amplitude of image and metaphor in *King Lear* is to study the dominant trope of division and separation which accompanies the various concepts of nature with which the play is concerned.

The tragedy begins as the Earl of Gloucester speaks with the Earl of Kent about "the division of the kingdom" (I. i. 3-4) that the King is proposing to make. Trumpets sound, and Lear enters in pomp and splendor at the head of a royal procession. A courtier unfurls a map of the realm as Goneril and the Duke of Albany, Regan and the Duke of Cornwall, Cordelia and her two suitors, the King of France and Duke of Burgundy, hearken to his speech:

> Know that we have divided
> In three our kingdom. And 'tis our fast intent
> To shake all cares and business from our age,
> Conferring them on younger strengths while we
> Unburdened crawl toward death.
>
> . . . .
>
> Tell me, my daughters,
> Since now we will divest us both of rule,
> Interest of territory, cares of state,
> Which of you shall we say doth love us most?
> That we our largest bounty may extend
> Where nature doth with merit challenge.   (I. i. 37ff.)

From this action the subsequent tragedy will unfold: Lear's division of the kingdom is a direct and willful abdication of monarchical responsibility, a breaking of political order, while his demand for the love test is a similar disruption of natural and moral bonds. Certainly the gravity of Lear's act would have been perceived by many in an audience in Shakespeare's day. The desirability of political

2

unity and stability, a good and virtuous king fulfilling the days of his reign, had been chronicled in innumerable *de casibus* tragedies of the Middle Ages, those narratives of the falls of famous men, and given even more emphatic form in the early Tudor *The Mirror for Magistrates* (1559) through didactic pronouncements about the nature of kingship.[8] As Eubulus, a character in *Gorboduc* (1561-1562), commented with shrewd political insight in that earliest of English tragedies:

> Within one land one single rule is best:
> Divided reigns do make divided hearts,
> But peace preserves the country and the prince.[9]

This statement reflects a set of philosophical and political assumptions that Shakespeare, a direct heir of the England of the Wars of the Roses, used recurrently in his tragedies of monarchy: the king is the anointed of the Lord; the state of his moral health and spiritual welfare will be mirrored in the realm he governs; his rule, ideally, should be one of justice and equity. In all instances, his function is to preserve fundamental order and stability so that those bonds which give order and meaning to human life may be strengthened and flourish. In his own being, the king is to govern his passions according to his reason: such governance will expand to the realm with which he has been entrusted. The Renaissance concepts of the microcosm-geocosm-macrocosm, as E. M. W. Tillyard has shown in *The Elizabethan World Picture* (Cambridge, 1943), are interrelated hierarchies and what affects one, beneficently or adversely, will be felt in others. In *King Lear* the monarch's "little world of man" (III. i. 10), the microcosm, is thrown into violent disorder; the geocosm, the natural world of the kingdom, mirrors a similar disorder, as does the macrocosm, the universe which encompasses the various worlds of the play.[10]

When Lear steps forward and seizes the golden coronet, bidding Albany and Cornwall to part it between them (I. i. 140-141), he embodies in his own soul a dichotomy between reasoned judgment and passionate fury. His act gives scope to the avarice of the elder daughters and leads to "division/Although as yet the face of it be covered/With mutual cunning, 'twixt Albany and Cornwall" (III. i. 19-21). The dissolution and disturbance spread to the cosmos itself in the storm scene as Lear entreats the winds and cataracts, sulphurous lightning and oak-cleaving thunderbolts to

> Smite flat the thick rotundity o' the world!
> Crack nature's molds, all germens spill at once
> That make ingrateful man!   (III. ii. 7-9)

Division and separation are pervasive in *King Lear*. Edmund scoffs at Gloucester's superstitious ramblings that the "late eclipses in the

3

sun and moon portend no good to us" (I. ii. 112ff.), yet the "sequent effects" the old Earl describes epitomize the drama:

> Love cools, friendship falls off, brothers divide. In cities, mutinies; in countries, discord; in palaces, treason; and the bond cracked 'twixt son and father. This villain of mine comes under the prediction, there's son against father. The King falls from bias of nature, there's father against child. We have seen the best of our time. Machinations, hollowness, treachery, and all ruinous disorders follow us disquietly to our graves. (I. ii. 115 ff.)

Throughout the entire tragedy resounds the gnomic rebuke of the Fool to the King:

> When thou clovest thy crown i' the middle and gavest
> away both parts, thou borest thine ass on thy back
> o'er the dirt. Thou hadst little wit in thy bald
> crown when thou gavest thy golden one away. (I. iv. 175-178)

The metaphoric truth of his statement infuses the total drama. Through Lear's lack of understanding, a kingdom has been cast away, and, as a result, ruinous disorders will follow many disquietly to their graves.

Many other passages in the play refer directly to division and separation. In thinking of the pride and vanity that led him to his folly, Lear recognizes that his "frame of nature" has been wrenched "from the fixed place" (I. iv. 290-291). The Earl of Gloucester whispers fearfully that "Our flesh and blood is grown so vile . . ./That it doth hate what gets it" (III. iv. 150-151). The Duke of Albany speaks in horror of nature dividing, condemning itself, and in the restoration scene between Lear and Cordelia the youngest daughter prays that the "kind gods" will

> Cure this great breach in his abusèd nature!
> The untuned and jarring senses, oh, wind up
> Of this child-changèd father! (IV. vii. 14-17)

After the blinded Gloucester is reconciled with Edgar, "his flawed heart—/. . . twixt two extremes of passion, joy and grief,/Burst smilingly" (V. iii. 196-199), while the death of the Earl of Kent, imminent as the play closes, is described with imagery that relates still further to division: "His grief grew puissant, and the strings of life/Began to crack" (V. iii. 216-217). When Lear enters the drama for the final time, carrying the dead Cordelia in his arms, he bids the spectators utter grief "That heaven's vault should crack" (V. iii. 259), and the realm that remains to be governed is seen as "the gored state" (V. iii. 320). Great breaches in nature, divided hearts in individual souls, unfilial divisions in families, and treasonous divisions in the kingdom—all are portrayed on a panoramic backdrop against which human suffering may make the vaults of heaven split.

4

Illuminating both the established Elizabethan-Jacobean beliefs in an interrelated hierarchy of moral, political, and natural order, and the Shakespearean fusion of the particular with the universal, this pattern of division lies at the center of the drama. Lear partitions the realm because of the division he makes in his mind between personal comfort and kingly responsibility; he reflects a serious division between reasoned judgment and vain passion, as well as a division in natural and moral bonds, when he stages the love test, a situation in which he demands natural family ties of affection to be controverted, and when he rashly disinherits and banishes Cordelia, the child who has aptly replied to his petulant demands:

> I love your Majesty
> According to my bond, nor more nor less.   (I. i. 94-95)

Bonds snapping asunder and dividing are obviously seen in the treasonous conspiracy of Regan and Goneril, the plotting of Edmund against Gloucester (his father) and Edgar (his half-brother), in the adulterous scheming of Goneril and the rivalry between her and Regan for possession of Edmund, and in the self-serving machinations of the faithless servant, Oswald, and the political opportunist, the courtier Curan. The very presence of Edmund, moreover, dramatically embodies a broken commitment and forsworn vow. He is, as Gloucester bawdily boasts in the first scene, a bastard son, a knave who "came something saucily into the world before he was sent for, yet . . . there was good sport at his making, and the whoreson must be acknowledged" (I. i. 21-24). Disruption, separation, and division of natural, moral, and political bonds, therefore, are dramatized in *King Lear* through metaphor and imagery which encompass the dividing strings of the broken heart, civil war within the kingdom, and mighty breaches within the cosmos itself.

Subsumed into this metaphoric pattern are explorations of the destructive and creative aspects of both moral and physical nature. The world that Lear envisions when he distributes his kingdom is fruitful, harmonious, and peaceful. He speaks of "shadowy forests and . . . champaigns riched,/With plenteous rivers and wide-skirted meads" (I. i. 65-66). The natural reality that he soon encounters, however, is far different. The head that wore a crown will "wage against the enmity o' the air/To be a comrade with the wolf and owl" (II. iv. 212-213). The king will be plummeted into a physical world of violent storms, barrenness, and darkness. "Alack, the night comes on," moans Gloucester, "and the bleak winds/Do sorely ruffle. For many miles about/There's scarce a bush" (II. iv. 302-304). Kingly robes and golden coronets, borne on velvet cushions, recede into memory as one of the Knights in Lear's retinue describes the monarch

5

Contending with the fretful elements.
Bids the wind blow the earth into the sea,
Or swell the curlèd waters 'bove the main,
That things might change or cease; tears his white hair,
Which the impetuous blasts, with eyeless rage,
Catch in their fury, and make nothing of;
Strives in his little world of man to outscorn
The to-and-fro-conflicting wind and rain.
This night, wherein the cub-drawn bear would couch,
The lion and the belly-pinchèd wolf
Keep their fur dry, unbonneted he runs,
And bids what will take all.   (III. i. 4-15)

The King who once had ruled in splendor will wander

As mad as the vexed sea, singing aloud,
Crowned with rank fumiter and furrow weeds,
With burdocks, hemlock, nettles, cuckoo flowers,
Darnel, and all the idle weeds that grow
In our sustaining corn.   (IV. iv. 2-6)

Rank and gross weeds appropriately form his crown at this point in
the play, for the realm itself has become barren, usurped by the
rapacious Regan and Goneril, and the chaos in Lear's mind is fittingly
likened to vexed seas, vast oceans tossed in disorder and conflict.[11]
The nature that Lear comes to see is that expressed by Edgar,
masquerading as Tom o' Bedlam, a world of "poor pelting villages,
sheepcotes and mills" (II. iii. 18), a world where the foul fiend

. . . gives the web and the pin, squints the eye and makes the harelip,
mildews the white wheat and hurts the poor creature of earth.
(III. iv. 121 ff.)

The words of the Bedlamite describe a physical reality where the
poor and mad are "led through fire and through flame, through
ford and whirlpool, o'er bog and quagmire," and forced to eat "the
swimming frog, the toad, the tadpole, the wall newt . . . cow dung
for sallets . . . the old rat and the ditch dog" and to drink "the
green mantle of the standing pool" (III. iv. 51ff.). The "dreadful
pother" (III. ii. 50) of the gods breaks over Lear's head—the elemental
fury of sheets of fire, bursts of horrid thunder, groans of roaring wind
and rain—and through it echoes the anguished cry of the beggar
in rags—"Tom's a-cold. . . . Tom's a-cold" (III. iv. 59ff.) and the
plaintive lament of the Fool that a great while ago the world began,
and "the rain it raineth every day" (III. ii. 74-77). Lear becomes en-
meshed in forces of destruction, and what Samuel Taylor Coleridge
perceptively described as "a world's *convention* of agonies"[12] in the
storm on the heath arises from the monarch's recognition of those
forces in the human spirit and the natural world which deprive,
destroy, blight, and wither.

6

Character groupings within the play further embody these patterns of destruction and creativity. Goneril, Regan, Edmund, Cornwall, and Oswald express barrenness and hatred: they are egocentric, shrewdly calculating, brutal and ruthless. They belong to a world of the barbarous and monstrous. They lack all capacity to love, and, appropriately enough, are afflicted with lustful sterility, an insatiable appetite for power and sensual experience that recognizes no bonds or limits and that is, ultimately, self-destroying. In contrast to them are Cordelia and Edgar, the faithful Kent, the loyal retinue of Knights, and the King of France, characters who are motivated by a respect for moral bonds and a love that is self-sacrificing, forgiving, and spiritually creative.

Clustered around Cordelia from the very beginning are images of fruitfulness and plenitude: she is the youngest and the fairest daughter, Lear's "joy," the child he has loved most, the one on whom he thought "to set [his] rest" (I. i. 84ff.). Cordelia is the daughter "to whose young love/The vines of France and milk of Burgundy/Strive to be interested" (I. i. 85-87). She becomes the wife of the King of France, a lord who sees immediately that "She is herself a dowry" and who knows well that

> Love's not love
> When it is mingled with regards that stand
> Aloof from the entire point.   (I. i. 241-243)

Fulfilling the multiple roles of loyal subject, faithful daughter, loving child, and virtuous wife, Cordelia comes to Dover with the powers of France in order to end the civil strife in Britain and to restore Lear to his rightful throne. Her motivation for returning to the kingdom, in contrast to her sisters' acts in seizing it, is never "blown ambition," but "love, dear love, and our aged father's right" (IV. iv. 27-28), and her faithfulness is further mirrored in Gloucester, who chooses at great personal cost to aid his King; in Kent, who, upon punishment of death if discovered, serves Lear throughout his sufferings; and in Edgar, unjustly accused and dispossessed, who seeks to comfort and restore Gloucester to his rightful place. From these characters come creative impulses of spirit—loyalty, endurance, faith, sacrifice, devotion, courage, love—which restore order and re-establish the bonds which are essential for stability, peace, and fruitfulness in all areas of human life.

In opposition to them are Regan and Goneril, Edmund and Cornwall, whose very presences invoke curses of blight (I. iv. 297ff.; II. iv. 281ff.), whose lives become sterile chaos, and whose kingdoms become realms of excess, cruelty, and unnaturalness. Fittingly enough, these characters belong to a world beset with violent storms and tempestuous seas. Under their governance, the kingdom becomes a wasteland, filled with nettles and hemlock, where idle weeds indeed choke out the sustaining corn (IV. iv. 1-6). Consistently seen as savage beings, they are likened to the most loathsome animals, plague-ridden and infected. At one point Lear describes Regan as

> . . . a disease that's in my flesh
> Which I must needs call mine. Thou art a boil,
> A plague sore, an embossed carbuncle,
> In my corrupted blood.   (II. iv. 225-228)

Goneril appears in her ingratitude as a "marble-hearted fiend," a horrible, sharp-toothed serpent (I. iv. 281ff.). Together they have tried to sink their "boarish fangs" into the "anointed flesh" of a king (III. vii. 58); they are "pernicious daughters" (III. ii. 22), "pelican daughters" (III. iv. 77), "doghearted daughters" (IV. iii. 47), possessed of natures in which murderous lechery is rampant. It is the Duke of Albany who turns in revulsion from Goneril and pronounces the most fitting statement on that nature which condemns its very origin:

> That nature which contemns it[s] origin
> Cannot be bordered certain in itself.
> She that herself will sliver and disbranch
> From her material sap, perforce must wither
> And come to deadly use.
>
> .   .   .   .
>
> Humanity must perforce prey on itself,
> Like monsters of the deep.   (IV. ii. 32ff.)

The cursed and the blessed, the chaotic and the ordered, the destructive and the creative—all receive full metaphoric and thematic treatment in *King Lear*.

Another complex world in the play is that of dramatic action. In many ways the tragedy is a swirling tempest of movement, interspersed with tableaux and choral commentaries. Soliloquy is used sparsely in *King Lear,* and, unlike other Shakespearean dramas, a number of characters consistently utter choral-like statements: the Fool, the Duke of Albany, Edgar, and Earl of Kent.[13] If five key episodes in the tragedy are considered, perhaps the nature and effect of action may be understood somewhat more clearly. These scenes include the division of the kingdom (I. i.), the storm on the heath (III. ii. and iv.), the mock trial (III. vi.), the mad rhapsody in the fields of Dover (IV. vi.), and the deaths of Lear and Cordelia (V. iii.).

As monarch and man, Lear "hath ever but slenderly known himself" (I. i. 296-297), and his propensity for rash action manifests itself in his determination to split the realm, the rapidity with which he bows to the flattery of Goneril and Regan, and the impetuous fit of proud anger that causes him to disown and banish Cordelia. Kent's courage-

8

ous reprimand against Lear's initial action has the tone of choral declaration and suggests as well a dramatic foreshadowing:

> What wouldst thou do, old man?
> Think'st thou that duty shall have dread to speak
> When power to flattery bows? To plainness honor's bound
> When majesty stoops to folly. Reverse thy doom,
> And in thy best consideration check
> This hideous rashness. (I. i. 148-153)

That Kent's fears have a sound basis in fact is proved almost immediately by the hurried conversation between Goneril and Regan as they gloat over Lear's "poor judgment" in casting off Cordelia, grant that "the best and soundest of his time hath been but rash," and resolve to ". . . hit together. . . . We must do something, and i' the heat" (I. i. 291ff.). This sense of movement is carried forward to where we next see Lear: the King is hunting with his Knights, and he has struck one of Goneril's servants for chiding the Fool. He is soon to be in a violent quarrel with Oswald, then Goneril, an action paralleled by his rapid departure from Albany's castle, his subsequent quarrel with Regan, and his flight into the storm. Interspersed throughout this quickly moving section are the Fool's oracular quips, statements which again sound a choral note and which precede the initial quarrel that breaks out between the King and Goneril:

> Truth's a dog must to kennel. He must be whipped
> out, when Lady the brach may stand by the fire and
> stink. (I. iv. 124-126)

> Thou hadst little wit in thy bald crown when thou
> gavest thy golden one away. (I. iv. 177-178)

> For you know, Nuncle,
> The hedge sparrow fed the cuckoo so long
> That it had it[s] head bit off by it[s] young. (I. iv. 234-236)

Furthermore, the angry haste with which he leaves Goneril's halls is juxtaposed against the telling warning of the Fool:

> Thou shouldst not have been old till thou
> hadst been wise. (I. v. 48-49)

Similarly, the quarrel with Regan is anticipated by the cryptic bitterness in the song the Fool chants to Lear as they enter Gloucester's castle and find the King's messenger (the disguised Earl of Kent) in the stocks:

> Fathers that wear rags
>   Do make their children blind,
> But fathers that bear bags
>   Shall see their children kind.
> Fortune, that arrant whore,
> Ne'er turns the key to the poor. (II. iv. 48-53)

> That sir which serves and seeks for gain,
>   And follows but for form,
> Will pack when it begins to rain,
>   And leave thee in the storm.   (II. iv. 79-82)

Throughout this portion as Lear flees from Goneril to Regan, then on to the heath, the words of Kent give still further generalization and choric commentary. As the disguised peer sits in the stocks, awaiting the arrival of the King, he contemplates the power of destinal forces over human life. "Fortune," he bids, "good night. Smile once more, turn thy wheel" (II. ii. 180). The mutations of the world, the power of Fortune to cast a monarch from high estate to low,[14] will be seen in the vivid dramatic action of the storm on the heath.

Both external and internal action and conflict are present on a massive scale in the scenes on the heath. The storm reinforces the sense of disorder in the soul, the kingdom, and the universe, thus fusing the realms of microcosm-geocosm-macrocosm. At the same time, the storm—external nature and the chaos therein—reinforces the internal psychological and spiritual upheavals that Lear is experiencing. The violent tempest, moreover, provides the moral reality that contributes toward Lear's growth in self-understanding. It is only in this night, recurrently described as too rough for nature to endure, that Lear begins to gain a deeper and wider knowledge of his own nature and past frailties:

> I tax not you, you elements, with unkindness.
> I never gave you kingdom, called you children,
> You owe me no subscription. Then let fall
> Your horrible pleasure. Here I stand, your slave,
> A poor, infirm, weak, and despised old man.   (III. ii. 16-20)

As he thinks of his own errors in judgment, he turns his mind toward those who cloak secret crimes and hidden lusts under a seemingly fair or just appearance:

>   Let the great gods,
> That keep this dreadful pother o'er our heads,
> Find out their enemies now. Tremble, thou wretch,
> That hast within thee undivulgèd crimes
> Unwhipped of justice. Hide thee, thou bloody hand,
> Thou perjured, and thou simular man of virtue
> That are incestuous. Caitiff, to pieces shake,
> That under covert and convenient seeming
> Hast practiced on man's life. Close pent-up guilts,
> Rive your concealing continents and cry
> These dreadful summoners grace. I am a man
> More sinned against than sinning.   (III. ii. 49-60)

Lear's growing self-awareness throughout the storm scene needs to be firmly acknowledged, for it, coupled with his determination to

10

gain in patience, precedes and is requisite for his growth in compassion. The proud ruler of the opening scene now stands on a storm-ridden heath and turns his thoughts from self to the Fool—"who labors to outjest/His heart-struck injuries" (III. i. 16-17)—who accompanies him:

> How dost, my boy? Art cold?
> I am cold myself.
> . . . .
> Poor fool and knave, I have one part in my heart
> That's sorry yet for thee. (III. ii. 69-73)

His strength to endure arises from a new found concern, a pity for the sufferings of another human being, a sense of remorse for past guilt and selfishness. Bidding the Fool to seek shelter in the hovel, Lear dwells not on his own personal sufferings but on those who have been afflicted with adversity within his kingdom:

> In, boy, go first. You houseless poverty—
> Nay, get thee in. I'll pray, and then I'll sleep.
> Poor naked wretches, wheresoe'er you are,
> That bide the pelting of this pitiless storm,
> How shall your houseless heads and unfed sides,
> Your looped and windowed raggedness, defend you
> From seasons such as these? Oh, I have ta'en
> Too little care of this! Take physic, pomp.
> Expose thyself to feel what wretches feel,
> That thou mayst shake the superflux to them
> And show the Heavens more just.   (III. iv. 26-36)

His prayer illumines the broadened sympathy that has come to his own spirit: his capacity to see is linked clearly to his ability to feel, and the tempest in his soul has enlightened the heart.

The problem of power and the nature of justice, concepts inherent in the passage and throughout the action in the heath section, are treated again in the mock trial (III. vi.) where Lear, whose wits have turned in the fury of the storm, arraigns Goneril and Regan while the Fool and Edgar, masked yet as Tom o' Bedlam, serve as magistrates. In the mad scene (IV. vi.) in the fields of Dover, moreover, dramatic action reaches a strong peak, and matters of justice are further explored.

The mock trial explicitly dramatizes the abstract ideas which form Lear's questioning of the nature of justice. The King, Edgar, Kent, and the Fool represent "houseless poverty" as they enter the ruined farmhouse, adjoining Gloucester's castle. Lear, sinking deeper into madness, calls to the bar for arraignment the forces that are consuming him and his kingdom. Disordered voices cry throughout the scene: the Fool chants that he will go to bed at noon, mad Tom shrieks for all to beware the foul fiend, and Lear, with deep

11

poignancy, dreams of the small pet dogs he once had at court and fears that they too have become vicious curs: "The little dogs and all,/Tray, Blanch, and Sweetheart, see, they bark at me" (III. vi. 65-66). Action is disjointed and swirling. Goneril and Regan, daughters of warped looks and warped hearts, are called to trial in the mind of the King. "Let us deal justly," sings Edgar (the Bedlam beggar). "Come, march to wakes and fairs and market towns" (III. vi. 42ff.). "Make no noise, make no noise," whispers Lear, "Draw the/curtains. So, so, so. We'll go to supper i' the morning" (III. vi. 89-91). Disorder and inversion are paramount within the scene. The "robèd man of justice" and his "yokefellow of equity" (III. vi. 38-39) preside over a chaotic movement that envelops the players and is not broken until Lear falls into a state of exhaustion. "Oppressèd nature sleeps," Kent says to Gloucester as the Earl warns him to take the King toward Dover (III. vi. 104ff.), and a quiet, choral commentary, spoken by Edgar, concludes the episode:

> When we our betters see bearing our woes,
> We scarcely think our miseries our foes.
>
> .   .   .   .
>
> How light and portable my pain seems now
> When that which makes me bend makes the King bow,
> He childed as I fathered!   (III. vi. 109-110, 115-117)

His calm statement is both a contrast and an intensification to the complex action that has preceded it.

When Lear next appears in the drama, he runs mad through the fields of Dover, dressed in tatters and crowned with weeds. He speaks of a world disordered, governed by lust and avarice. In his vision he sees the farmer's dog bark at the beggar, and the creature run from the cur:

>   There
> thou mightst behold the great image of authority.
> A dog's obeyed in office.   (IV. vi. 161-163)

The fair appearance, hiding the foul reality, obsesses his mind:

> Thou rascal beadle, hold thy bloody hand!
> Why dost thou lash that whore? Strip thine own back.
> Thou hotly lust'st to use her in that kind
> For which thou whip'st her. The usurer hangs the cozener.
> Through tattered clothes small vices do appear,
> Robes and furred gowns hide all. Plate sin with gold
> And the strong lance of justice hurtless breaks.
> Arm it in rags, a pigmy's straw does pierce it.   (IV. vi. 164-171)

The entire scene revolves around the meeting between the old King and the blinded Gloucester, and, in the midst of sweeping action, the pathos of the situation is chorically expressed by Edgar:

12

THEATRVM VI-
TÆ HVMANÆ.

CAPVT I.

VITA HVMANA EST TANQVAM
Theatrum omnium miſeriarum.

Vita hominis tanquam circus, vel grande theatrum est:
Quod tragici oſtentat cunɗa referta metus.
Hoc laſciva caro, peccatum, morſque, Satanque
Triſti hominem vexant, exagitantque modo.

Plate 1   Life as a Theatre from Jean Boissard's *Theatrum Vitae Humanae* (1596).

Thou must be patient, we came crying hither.
Thou know'st the first time that we smell the air,
We wawl and cry. I will preach to thee. Mark.
. . . .
When we are born, we cry that we are come
To this great stage of fools.   (*King Lear*, IV. vi. 182-187)

13

> I would not take this from report. It is,
> And my heart breaks at it.   (IV. vi. 144-145)

The King grants that one may see how this world goes with no eyes, and bids Gloucester hearken to his preaching:

> Thou must be patient, we came crying hither.
> Thou know'st the first time that we smell the air,
> We wawl and cry. I will preach to thee. Mark.
> .   .   .   .
> When we are born, we cry that we are come
> To this great stage of fools.   (IV. vi. 182-187)

The theatrical metaphor for human life which Lear expresses here is indeed fit setting for "the great image of authority" with which Shakespeare is concerned. Significantly enough, the passage is followed by the entrance of the Gentleman Knight who echoes Edgar's agonized observation, yet, at the same time, acknowledges those forces which offset rampant human evil:

> A sight most pitiful in the meanest wretch,
> Past speaking of in a king! Thou hast one daughter
> Who redeems nature from the general curse
> Which twain have brought her to.   (IV. vi. 208-211)

That redemption, a force which creates and preserves, brings order out of chaos and harmony out of dissonance, centers solely on the capacity to love, the observance of the bond which joins Cordelia to her King, father, state, and wedded lord. It is an active commitment to those "offices of nature" which are an established, immutable part of the thick rotundity of the world which stands firm and endures.

The final action of the drama depicts the old King with the body of the dead Cordelia in his arms. In the midst of grief and sorrow, Lear retains yet strength and royalty. He is, as Albany recognizes, "this old Majesty" (V. iii. 299), and his voice speaks not only with a heartbreaking pathos for his personal suffering, but also with an expansive concern for all human agony in the face of death:

> She's gone forever!
> I know when one is dead and when one lives.
> She's dead as earth.   (V. iii. 259-261)

As Lear feels death upon him, he entreats Edgar to loosen the clasps on his robe. We may recall that in the tempestuous storm scene when the King saw man as naked, unaccommodated, and alone, he tore off his clothes as he realized that he, himself, was also "such a poor, bare, forked animal" (III. iv. 111). The bond of mortality which linked together King and Bedlam beggar on the heath is affirmed once more as Lear experiences the finality of death. As

14

the scene demonstrates, the final action of all men is the embrace of death, and the words of the aged, blind Gloucester, spoken when he met the King in the fields of Dover, may echo in our consciousness:

> O ruined piece of nature! This great world
> Shall so wear out to naught.   (IV. vi. 137-138)

The actors who perform on this great stage of fools—those who have indeed shown the age and time its proper form and feature—are stilled by death. Again to Albany is given a choral commentary as the death march is played:

> The weight of this sad time we must obey,
> Speak what we feel, not what we ought to say,
> The oldest hath borne most. We that are young
> Shall never see so much, nor live so long.   (V. iii. 323-326)

The statement that Albany makes emphasizes for one final time what the major patterns of movement have been. As Francis Fergusson has observed, upon the dramatic action in *King Lear* rests much of the aesthetic and moral impact of the tragedy:

> But the form and meaning of the play as a whole are not to be found
> in the speeches of the characters, however profound and moving, but
> only in the relationships between them, and in the movement of the
> story. Shakespeare could identify himself with each character, yet at
> the same time move back, as it were, to see him objectively, and plan
> his role in the play. He was a master of 'plot' in Aristotle's sense of
> the word: by the arrangement of the incidents he gives the action
> its embodiment, meaning, and form. He saw the fundamental action
> (or motive) of the play as an attempt, more or less conscious, more or
> less wise or wicked, to find the natural order in Lear's anarchic Britain.
> From the contrasting visions of the characters arise their terrible con-
> flicts; and their conflicts (plus the incalculable element of chance)
> move the story to its conclusion. When some sort of order is restored,
> the action is complete, and the play is over.[15]

Albany's concluding declaration, therefore, is a comment which reflects both personal emotion and poised resolution. The actions of those who have spoken what they felt, not what they ought to have said, comprise the substance of the drama: the major pattern of movement evolves from chaos to order.

In the world of action in *King Lear,* balance and symmetry in structure are apparent. Lear's banishment and disinheritance of Cordelia are paralleled not only by his exile of Kent, but also by Gloucester's banishment of Edgar. Ironically, the pattern is further emphasized by the actions of Regan and Goneril, Cornwall and Edmund. Lear is stripped of his last remnants of monarchy—the faithful retinue of Gentlemen Knights—and thrust into the storm. Gloucester, betrayed by Edmund, and blinded, is similarly thrust out of his own castle and dispossessed of his power. The acts of the

Plate 2   The Cycle of Life. A *Memento Mori* print
by Hans Schäufelein, ca. 1517.

World, world, O world!
But that thy strange mutations make us hate thee,
Life would not yield to age.   (*King Lear,* IV. i. 10-12)

Reprinted from Samuel Claggett Chew, *The Pilgrimage of Life* (New Haven, 1962) by permission of Yale University Press.

daughters, recapitulated by the machinations of Edmund, contrast to the deeds of the faithful children, Cordelia and Edgar. As Theodore Spencer has so lucidly demonstrated, intensification and amplification reign: the main plot of Lear and his daughters is balanced by the subplot of Gloucester and his sons.[16] We have not one evil daughter, but two; not one aged father, cruelly treated, but two. Even the servants are set in symmetrical arrangements: Kent, "an honest mind and plain—he must speak truth" (II. ii. 105) directly contrasts to Oswald, cleverly described as a "composition of a knave, beggar, coward, pander, and the son and heir of a mongrel bitch" (II. ii. 21-23). The parallelism is explicit.

16

Balanced and symmetrical action may be observed within individual acts and scenes and within the drama as a whole. After the division of the kingdom, Goneril and Regan immediately resolve to use to their advantage (I. i. 307ff.) Lear's lack of good judgment and propensity for rashness. Similarly, Edmund revels in the knowledge that he has "A credulous father, and a brother noble/Whose nature is so far from doing harms/That he suspects none. . . ." and vows to have lands by wit if not by birth (I. ii. 195-197). In the storm on the heath Lear gains the patience to bear his sufferings. His courage—reflected in his declaration, "Pour on, I will endure" (III. iv. 18)—finds intensification in Gloucester's similarly strengthened ability to endure in adversity:

> Henceforth I'll bear
> Affliction till it do cry out itself
> 'Enough, enough,' and die. (IV. vi. 75-77)

Lear's vision of social justice, moreover, receives amplification in Gloucester's awareness of inequity. The King cries,

> Take physic, pomp.
> Expose thyself to feel what wretches feel,
> That thou mayst shake the superflux to them
> And show the Heavens more just. (III. iv. 33-36)

while the Earl declares :

> Heavens, deal so still!
> Let the superfluous and lust-dieted man,
> That slaves your ordinance, that will not see
> Because he doth not feel, feel your power quickly.
> So distribution should undo excess
> And each man have enough. (IV. i. 69-74)

On all levels in the drama this sense of symmetrical action exists. Attached to Lear and Cordelia are the faithful Earl of Kent and the Gentlemen Knights. The loyal Kent, bearing just letters, is set against the scheming Oswald, carrying false accusations. The ruthless servants who aid Cornwall and Regan in the blinding of Gloucester are offset by the compassionate ones who minister to the old Earl. Lear's reconciliation with Cordelia has its counterpart in Edgar's reunion with Gloucester and his later exchange of forgiveness with Edmund. The choleric Cornwall emphasizes the savagery of Goneril and Regan, and, in addition, becomes a contrast to the meditative Duke of Albany.

The beginning and the conclusion of *King Lear* perhaps best illustrate this sense of symmetrical action. The opening scene of the play is much like a tableau as Lear sweeps into the royal hall to the sound of trumpets and dramatically stations himself by the

17

unfurled map of the realm as the three daughters, the Dukes of Albany and Cornwall, the suitors of Cordelia, Gloucester and his sons, the Earl of Kent, and assembled courtiers stand poised for the action which is to ensue. The final scene of the play again suggests a dramatic tableau, but now the flourish of sennets is replaced by the muffled sounds of a death march. The three daughters are dead, joined in a final bond of silence. The Earl of Gloucester, as Edgar reports, has succumbed to death, and the Earl of Kent, with another journey shortly to go, has come "To bid my King and master aye good night" (V. iii. 235). With tragic poignancy, the major motifs with which the drama opened are repeated for a final time. The sorrowing Lear bends over Cordelia, hoping that her breath will stain a mirror or that her lips will stir a feather, and whispers, "Her voice was ever soft,/Gentle and low, an excellent thing in woman" (V. iii. 272-273), and we recall the Cordelia of the first scene who could not heave her heart into her mouth, the daughter who knew that she would "love, and be silent" (I. i. 63). The voice "whose low sound/Reverbs no hollowness" (I. i. 155-156) is breathless, and again, and for a far different reason, she cannot speak.

From minute, particular actions to a vast, sweeping panorama of movement, the symmetrical and the balanced structure *King Lear*. The pattern is indeed appropriate for those who have taken upon themselves "the mystery of things" (V. iii. 16), and allied themselves with those destinal powers who, in action beyond human comprehension, have worn out

> . . . pacts and sects of great ones
> That ebb and flow by the moon. (V. ii. 18-19)

King Lear is a drama of the human spirit, and one of the basic ways in which Shakespeare portrays Lear's change from a proud, irresponsible king to a man who has increased in wisdom and compassion is through the use of question. Fulfilling a dramatic, rhetorical, and moral function, questions ring through the play. In addition, they frequently embody the four central paradoxes around which the drama is formed: sight in blindness, reason in madness, wisdom in folly, and freedom in service.[17]

Dramatically, questions throw into sharp relief major conflicts and tensions. "What shall Cordelia do?" (I. i. 63), asks the youngest daughter to herself as she listens to the deceitful protestations of Regan and Goneril. "What can you say to draw/A third more opulent than your sisters?" (I. i. 87-88), Lear pompously demands. Upon Cordelia's simple reply that she loves him according to her bond, nor more nor less, come a series of angry responses from the King:

18

Nothing!   (I. i. 90)
But goes thy heart with this?   (I. i. 107)
So young and so untender?   (I. i. 108)

When Kent interposes—literally stepping between the dragon and his wrath—personal conflict is dramatized in his forceful, blunt interrogation:

What wouldst thou do, old man?
Think'st thou that duty shall have dread to speak
When power to flattery bows?   (I. i. 148-150)

Moreover, as Edmund rationalizes the ruse he is perpetrating on his father and half-brother, he speaks in a way that not only makes explicit his personal motivations but also sharply delineates essential lines of conflict:

Wherefore should I
Stand in the plague of custom, and permit
The curiosity of nations to deprive me,
For that I am some twelve or fourteen moonshines
Lag of a brother? Why bastard? Wherefore base?
When my dimensions are as well compact,
My mind as generous and my shape as true,
As honest madam's issue?   (I. ii. 2-9)

Lear's quarrel with Goneril, followed by another with Regan, is aptly caught, as we have noted, in the King's stunned realization, "Yea, is it come to this?" (I. iv. 326). The conflict will be intensified further as the two sisters cruelly bait the old King in their determination to deprive him of his knights and leave him totally helpless:

What need you five and twenty, ten, or five,
.   .   .   .
What need one?   (II. iv. 264, 267)

The "unnatural dealing" (III. iii. 2-3) that casts the King into the storm and rends the realm with civil war is emblematized as Lear dwells on monstrous ingratitude and asks,

Is it not as this mouth should tear this hand
For lifting food to 't?   (III. iv. 15-16)

Even Cordelia, waiting for Lear to awaken from a healing sleep, keeps this sense of dramatic conflict paramount through question:

Was this a face
To be opposed against the warring winds?
To stand against the deep dread-bolted thunder?
In the most terrible and nimble stroke
Of quick, cross lightning?
.   .   .   .
               . . . and wast thou fain, poor Father,
To hovel thee with swine and rogues forlorn
In short and musty straw?   (IV. vii. 31ff.)

And at the conclusion Lear's final question—"Do you see this? Look on her, look, her lips,/Look there, look there!" (V. iii. 310-311)—as he gazes toward the dead Cordelia forcefully embodies the creative and destructive realities of life which the tragedy has explored.[18]

Rhetorically, questions elaborate and amplify major themes, images, and metaphors. One example may perhaps suffice. A major image pattern of the play expresses the "boarish fangs" (III. vii. 58) of an evil nature. Immediately preceding mad Tom's recital in the storm scene of the sins of excess and lust is the starkly simple question posed by the King: "What hast thou been?" (III. iv. 86). The reply of the beggar is vivid in its intensity: "False of heart, light of ear, bloody of hand, hog in sloth, fox in stealth, wolf in greediness, dog in madness, lion in prey" (III. iv. 94-97). Lear listens to the bestial category—an apt enough delineation of one aspect of human nature within the tragedy—and asks searchingly, "Is man no more than this?" (III. iv. 106). That the question is answered through Lear's presence on the heath is a commonplace of Shakespearean criticism,[19] but the very statement, as so often in the drama, leads the reader to see through the richness of imagery and metaphor that vision of man's nature which recognizes simultaneously his highest nobility and his lowest degradation.

In the realm of moral and spiritual values, questions assume their greatest importance: they trace Lear's growth from egocentric, petulant anger to compassionate patience and love. From the moment the King divides the realm, he is set on a journey toward self-knowledge and deeper human understanding. Early in the course of the play the King begins to perceive "a most faint neglect of late" (I. iv. 73-74) in Goneril's household. He listens intently to the riddling lyrics, frequently expressed as questions, of the Fool. "Can you make no use of nothing, Nuncle?" (I. iv. 143-144), asks the Fool, only to be told by the King in a tone of reflective somberness, "Why, no, boy, nothing can be made out of nothing" (I. iv. 145-146). With paradoxical irony, Lear entreats the fool to teach him the meaning of folly. "Dost thou know the difference, my boy, between a bitter fool and a sweet fool?" (I. iv. 151-152), and the Fool, with unmistakable intent, dramatizes monarchical folly in the song that he sings:

> The lord that counseled thee
>   To give away thy land,
> Come place him here by me,
>   Do thou for him stand.
> The sweet and bitter fool
>   Will presently appear—
> The one in motley here,
>   The other found out there.   (I. iv. 154-161)

20

Questioning statement led to the song, as it does to Lear's pained response upon hearing the lyric, "Dost thou call me fool, boy?" (I. iv. 162). The Fool's reply is emphatic: "All thy other titles thou hast given away./That thou wast born with" (I. iv. 163-164). If all men, from king to beggar, are born with the title of fool, their lives, of necessity, become a search for self-awareness.

Perhaps for this reason, questions of identity are posed almost immediately in the tragedy. In a futile attempt to preserve his royal authority, Lear addresses Oswald: "Who am I, sir?" (I. iv. 86). The reply of the knavish steward smacks with insolence: "My lady's father." (I. iv. 87). Lear's numb incredulity at Goneril's insults leads him to question plaintively, "Who is it that can tell me who I am?" (I. iv. 250), and in response to his statement, the Fool answers with wisdom, "Lear's shadow" (I. iv. 251). The movement from surface insubstantiality (the shadow world of false vows, hollow protests, and hypocritical affirmations) to inward reality is beginning. By the time Lear stands on the heath, he knows that he has been a monarch who has neglected the cares of his realm, and when he strides through the fields of Dover, clad in tatters and crowned with weeds, he knows well, even in madness, that he is not ague-proof but is yet every inch a king. Lear's recognition of his own human frailty and his acceptance of past guilt for his actions against Cordelia and Kent, as well as his wider neglect of monarchical responsibility, lead to the remorse which expresses itself in concern for a fellow human being. In the storm scene, as we have seen, he speaks to the Fool as they approach the hovel in which they will find refuge, and his statement, significantly, takes the form of question: "How dost my boy? Art cold?" (III. ii. 68). Lear has sought to be "the pattern of all patience" (III. ii. 37), and compassion, not pride, emerges in his nature. His concern for the Fool is further manifested in his insistence that the lad enter the hovel first: "Nay, get thee in. I'll pray, and then I'll sleep" (III. iv. 27). Immediately following this gesture of love for the Fool occurs the "Poor naked wretches" speech, a key passage in regard to Lear's growth in moral stature and a declaration that is organized around direct questions:

> How shall your houseless heads and unfed sides,
> Your looped and windowed raggedness, defend you
> From seasons such as these? Oh, I have ta'en
> Too little care of this! (III. iv. 30-33)

The King's pondering of social injustice receives ironic emphasis as Edgar, disguised as mad Tom and accompanied by the terrified Fool, bounds out from the hovel. Again, the question that Lear asks as he looks at and listens to the scene before him becomes central to the drama and the Shakespearean tragic vision:

> Is man no more than this? (III. iv. 106)

We have suggested earlier that King Lear answers his question by his very presence on the heath—his endurance, his compassion, his capacity to love, his new-found humility, and his deepening knowledge of self. It is, paradoxically, the total recognition of man's frailty, limitation, and weakness that gives rise to an equal recognition of the human potential for strength, nobility, and dignity.[20]

That the harshness and severity of the storm have been stressed again and again is not coincidental. Gloucester shudders with awe as he learns that the King has fled to the heath (II. iv. 302-304). The Knight gives a vivid description of the elemental fury that lashes the land as Lear "Strives in his little world of man to outscorn/The to-and-fro-conflicting wind and rain" (III. i. 10-11). The King himself speaks an apostrophe to the violent weather, the roaring winds and rain and lightning that cleaves the strongest oak (III. ii. 1ff.). Kent broods in fear that the night is so tyrannous that nature cannot endure (III. iv. 2-3). Cornwall speaks of the unrestrained fury of the storm, and the Fool perceives that "Here's a night pities neither wise man nor fool" (III. ii. 12-13). Against this natural cataclysm, emblematic certainly of the moral and political cataclysm of the drama, Lear does stand, and he endures. In the height of his own agony, he turns from self-pity to a broad involvement with a suffering humanity, and his sympathy and knowledge lead him to ponder more deeply the nature of justice and power as he moves to the mock arraignment of Regan and Goneril in a subsequent scene. The question "Is man no more than this?" leads directly to another inquiry which gives focus to the entire mock trial: "Is there any cause in nature/that makes these hard hearts?" (III. vi. 81-82). That Lear endures and that he questions affirm human worth and the human capacity to find meaning in suffering.[21] We do well, perhaps, to recall that Cordelia marvels that her father has survived his afflictions (IV. vii. 41-42) and that Kent stands in sorrowful awe at the conclusion of the tragedy as he looks upon Lear in death and pronounces a quiet and most perceptive benediction: "The wonder is he hath endured so long" (V. iii. 316). His statement is all the more emphatic in its somber weight, perhaps, for the interrogative framework which gives it its context.

Questions are also used extensively in the climactic mad scene for the purpose of making moral statement:

> See how yond Justice rails upon yond simple thief. . . . Change places and, handy-dandy, which is the Justice, which is the thief? Thou hast seen a farmer's dog bark at a beggar? . . . And the creature run from the cur? (IV. vi. 154ff.)

At this point in the play Edgar comments on the reasoned voice that speaks through the mad exterior: "Oh, matter and impertinency mixed!/Reason in madness!" (IV. vi. 178-179). Along with sight in blindness, wisdom in folly, and freedom in service, reason in madness becomes a major paradox in *King Lear*. Those who are mad— seemingly or genuinely—utter profound truths on the nature of the human condition. Those who stumbled when they saw perceive realities and gain spiritual illumination only when they lose physical sight or are able to move beyond the deceptive surfaces surrounding them. Those whose words appear to be folly understand intuitively the highest kinds of wisdom. Those who truly serve because of the bond which binds them to others are those who find true freedom in human commitment and love.

Intensifying these motifs still further is disguise—Edgar as a Bedlam beggar, the Earl of Kent as a servant. Those whose honesty should need no cloak are forced to hide. Again, the words of the Fool ring clear—

> Truth's a dog that must to kennel. He must
> be whipped out, when Lady the brach may stand
> by the fire and stink.   (I. iv. 124-126)

The image of authority, the disorder and injustice that Lear questions and understands in madness, is exactly this, for one segment of the moral world of the tragedy demonstrates that a cur is obeyed in office and robes and furred gowns hide all.

Indispensable to a similar pattern of growth of understanding in Gloucester are the questions which Edgar asks:

> Oh gods! Who is't can say 'I am
>   at the worst'?
> I am worse than e'er I was.
>
> .   .   .   .   .   .
> And worse I may be yet. The worst
>   is not
> So long as we can say 'This is the worst.'   (IV. i. 27-30)
>
> What, in ill thoughts again? Men must endure
> Their going hence, even as their coming hither.
> Ripeness is all.   (V. ii. 9-11)

If questions are used to point toward the purification through suffering and increased wisdom that Lear and Gloucester attain, they also relate to personal reconciliation and re-establishment of order.

When Cordelia addresses Lear in the French camp near Dover, she speaks in a manner which reasserts the order of her bond as subject and daughter and which brings together the divided breach in the kingdom and the heart:

> How does my royal lord? How fares your Majesty?   (IV. vii. 44)

Lear's unbelieving sense of wonder and joy at the sight of the child whom he loves and has so grievously wronged leads him to question first whether he is on a hellish wheel of fire and Cordelia a saint in bliss (IV. vii. 45-48), and next, whether he is in Britain at all:

> Where have I been? Where am I? Fair daylight?
> . . . .
> Am I in France?   (IV. vii. 52ff.)

Kent's simple reply has profound significance—"In your own kingdom, sir" (IV. vii. 77)—and is amplified by the doctor's comment: "The great rage,/You see, is killed in him" (IV. vii. 78-79).[22] The forgiving love of Cordelia and Kent, along with Lear's own penitence, has brought about this restoration, and questions have made more intense the moral explorations of the scene.

In *King Lear* we see simultaneously two forces in the human spirit: the destructive and the creative, the evil and the good. Questions have consistently emphasized these polarities. One of the final questions that Lear poses—perhaps one of the most important—rests upon one aspect of the destructive. As he holds Cordelia in the final scene, he speaks:

> Why should a dog, a horse, a rat, have life
> And thou no breath at all? Thou'lt come no more,
> Never, never, never, never, never!   (V. iii. 306-308)

At this same time Kent asks, "Is this the promised end?" and Edgar echoes, "Or image of that horror?" (V. iii. 263-264). We in turn ask ourselves if the conclusion of the play is nothing more than unrelieved horror and loss, "cheerless, dark, and deadly" (V. iii. 290), or if, in some sense, justice is affirmed. The most rapacious evil has consumed itself—Goneril, Regan, Cornwall, and Edmund—but the sufferings of the innocent, the guiltless Cordelia, loom large. Edgar, we recall, had assured his father and Edmund that the gods were just,[23] but now he recoils in fear and pity at the sight before him.

It may be suggested, perhaps, that it is not so much Cordelia's death that the tragic poet may be questioning here, but rather the quality of the life that has preceded it. That the event creates a terrible sense of waste and loss, of anguish and grief, is a fact that speaks eloquently of that love which redeems nature from the general curse, a quality of spirit which is all the more valuable because it is vulnerable and fragile. That which was ordered and harmonious has been destroyed, but the destruction does not lessen either the morally sound and creative force which existed with vigor and vibrancy in Cordelia or the basic reality of the qualities of heart that she possessed. Through her return to the state, Lear is spiritually healed and restored, and some semblance of political

24

Plate 3   Time and the Seasons from the *Emblemata* of Otho Vaenius (1612).

Men must endure
Their going hence, even as their coming hither.
Ripeness is all.   (*King Lear*, V. ii. 9-11)

25

order, albeit tenuous, ordained within the kingdom. Lear's question, therefore, becomes yet another stage in his understanding of human mortality. He was every inch a king only when he realized that he had taken too little care for his realm and that he was not ague-proof. His entry into the kingdom of death is the final experience that he undergoes in his ever-expanding knowledge of human existence. His first question, we remember, was proud, self-centered, and vain:

> Which of you shall we say doth love us most?   (I. i. 52)

His final question measures the amount of compassion, humility, and human involvement that he has attained:

> Why should a dog, a horse, a rat, have life
> And thou no breath at all?   (V. iii. 306-307)

In the utter simplicity of his question is, perhaps, that human awareness that makes the ending of the tragedy the Shakespearean grand dirge for human suffering.

Certainly much of the sustained power of the conclusion rests upon the intensity of question after question, posed to spectator and reader as the great world of the drama indeed wears out to naught. "I will catechize the world . . . ," once spoke another Shakespearean figure in *Othello*, "that is, make questions, and by them answer" (III. iv. 16-17). In *King Lear* a world has been catechized through questions, and the silent answers of those who love remain as a redemptive reality whose vital breath forms a timeless statement of human majesty.

In the various worlds that *King Lear* envisions, man himself is at the center of things and chooses, as Pico Della Mirandola once wrote, whether to incline toward that which is blessed or that which is cursed:

> We have set thee at the world's center that thou mayest from thence more easily observe whatever is in the world. We have made thee neither of heaven nor of earth, neither mortal nor immortal, so that with freedom of choice and with honor, as though the maker and molder of thyself, thou mayest fashion thyself in whatever shape thou shalt prefer. Thou shalt have the power to degenerate into the lower forms of life, which are brutish. Thou shalt have the power, out of thy soul's judgment, to be reborn into the higher forms, which are divine.[24]

Freedom of the will, freedom to choose, needs to be acknowledged here, for this choice, along with this conception of man, gives tragic tension and import to Shakespearean tragedy as indeed it has to the tragic spirit within the Classical-Judeo-Christian tradition. Early in the play Edmund boasts that it is "the surfeit of our own behavior" that often makes us "sick in Fortune" (I. ii. 128-130), and against his comment those passages by Gloucester and Kent (IV. i. 38-39 and IV. iii. 34-37) which indict the gods as responsible for man's sufferings should be placed. Nature's molds, as Lear comes to realize, are capable of producing a Cordelia or a Goneril, an Edmund or an Edgar, yet it is clearly the surfeit of Lear's pride and Gloucester's folly that first unleashes the forces of destructive evil which plague the kingdom.

King Lear is not, then, a drama of unrelieved pessimism and despair. It possesses rather the human grandeur and tragic magnitude which ennoble and give meaning to mortal suffering. If one part of man's nature may be depraved and monstrously fiendish, another may be rational, ordered, and redemptively blessed. Lear's agony at Cordelia's death is human pathos—an ultimate expression of grief and sorrow—but it does not take away from the significance of that death, brought about by a spirit of love and forgiveness which would hazard all danger in order to fulfill its proper "offices of nature." The play, consequently, maintains a dramatic tension which remains taut as it contemplates man as a being who freely chooses between those forces which create and those which destroy.

We study *King Lear*, however, not as an isolated Renaissance tragedy but as a consummate work of art within the humanistic tradition.[25] Of all the realms that the tragedy illumines, perhaps that of the humanistic vision is the most important, for in the drama is found the thematic continuity that runs through the greatest literary achievements of our Western heritage. In its exploration of pride and power, of justice and love, of wisdom and endurance, *King Lear* forcefully dramatizes that in the examined life alone man is able to discern the ultimate realities which shape his world.

The voice heard in Shakespeare's most profound drama sustains a tone heard first on those plains of Troy where the misery of the human condition was given epic scope:

> .   .   .   among all creatures that breathe on earth
> and crawl on it
> there is not anywhere a thing more dismal than man is.[26]

The vexed seas of Shakespeare's Lear crashed also on that other voyager whose endurance in adversity is expressed in his somber reflections on the frailty of all men:

> Of mortal creatures, all that breathe and move,
> earth bears none frailer than mankind. What man
> believes in woe to come, so long as valor and
> tough knees are supplied him by the gods? But
> when the gods in bliss bring miseries on, then
> willy-nilly, blindly, he endures. Our minds are as
> the days are, dark or bright, blown over by the
> father of gods and men.[27]

The weight of the sad time that must be obeyed in human mortality is indeed similar, whether in Homeric epic or Renaissance tragedy.

The themes expressed in Shakespeare's play are in harmony with an Hebraic spirit that laments

> Man *that* is born of a woman *is* of few days, and
>   full of trouble.
> He cometh forth like a flower, and is cut down: he
>   fleeth also as a shadow, and continueth not.
>
> .   .   .   .
>
> Yet man is born unto trouble, as the sparks
>   fly upward.[28]

Yet the chord that is struck in this Jacobean tragedy contains many tonal modulations. When Lear recognizes his own guilt and frailty, speaking of woe that too late repents and reproaching himself for taking too little care of his monarchical responsibilities, we may think of another king, proud and rash, who learned through his sufferings on the royal throne of Thebes that "The greatest griefs are those we cause ourselves."[29] In other Greek tragedy we find also celebrated the heroic spirit that bears guilt and endures so that all might see that the life of man is often to be pitied, but

> To learn by suffering is the equation of Justice.[30]

For Shakespeare, Fortune placed Lear on a great stage of fools. For another tragedian, Zeus was the god

> Who setting us on the road
> Made this a valid law—
>   'That men must learn by suffering.'
> Drop by drop in sleep upon the heart
> Falls the laborious memory of pain,
> Against one's will comes wisdom;
> The grace of the gods is forced on us
> Throned inviolably.[31]

When Edgar poignantly thinks of the mutability of the world, the transitory nature of life and beauty, he is not far in spirit from the poet of Ecclesiastes:

> *One* generation passeth away, and *another* generation cometh:
>   but the earth abideth for ever.
> The sun also ariseth, and the sun goeth down, and hasteth
>   to his place where he arose.
> The wind goeth toward the south, and turneth about unto
>   the north; it whirleth about continually, and the
>   wind returneth again according to his circuits.
> All the rivers run into the sea; yet the sea *is* not full;
>   unto the place from whence the rivers come, thither
>   they return again.
>
> .   .   .   .
>
> The thing that hath been, it *is that* which shall be;
>   and that which is done *is that* which shall be done:
>   and *there is* no new *thing* under the sun.
>
> .   .   .   .

> And I gave my heart to know wisdom, and to know madness
> and folly: I perceived that this also is vexation of spirit.
> For in much wisdom is much grief: and he that increaseth
> wisdom increaseth sorrow.[32]

If men must endure the mutability of all things and gain wisdom through grief, as *King Lear* shows, they are aptly described in their going hence and coming hither in the poetry of still another choral ode:

> Alas for the seed of men.
>
> What measure shall I give these generations
> That breathe on the void and are void
> And exist and do not exist?
>
> Who bears more weight of joy
> Than mass of sunlight shifting in images,
> Or who shall make his thought stay on
> That down time drifts away?[33]

The human preoccupation with the drifting of time is heard still in the writings of a Roman emperor and Stoic philosopher. "In human life," commented Marcus Aurelius, "time is but a point, reality a flux, perception indistinct, the composition of the body subject to easy corruption, the soul a spinning top, fortune hard to make out, fame confused. To put it briefly: physical things are but a flowing stream, things of the soul dreams and vanity; life is but a struggle and a visit to a strange land. . . ."[34] The recognition of the temporal limitations of existence is constant in the humanistic tradition to which *King Lear* belongs. The wheel of Fortune—"our lady of Permutations"[35] as Dante once called her—turns incessantly within the tragedy and comes full circle within the transience of time.

Still other tones echo, however. We recall that Cordelia declares that she goes about her father's business in the realm (IV. iv. 23-24) and that she possesses a love which casts out all fear. If Lear asks, "Is man no more than this?" he is perhaps refashioning the question of the psalmist, "What is man, that thou art mindful of him? and the son of man, that thou visitest him?"[36] or restating the anguished inquiry of Job, "What *is* man, that thou shouldest magnify him? and that thou shouldest set thine heart upon him?"[37] For the Hebrew poet and the Jacobean tragedian, these questions are perhaps unanswerable. The human image that we see in *King Lear* is both wondrously and fearfully made, and the tragic riddle that is posed, like that of the Sphinx, deals with mysteries in the nature of man. "Numberless are the world's wonders," chants the chorus in Sophocles' *Antigone,* "but none more wonderful than man."[38] Wonder is perhaps the most appropriate term to apply to Shakespeare's tragedy: wonder at the complex richness of the worlds it contains, wonder

29

that Lear did indeed endure so long, wonder at the presence of a Cordelia, wonder at the certainties of creation and destruction within human life. In its totality, the play possesses that sense of awe found in the most famous of the classical choral odes:

> Numberless are the world's wonders, but none
> More wonderful than man; the stormgray sea
> Yields to his prows, the huge crests bear him high;
> Earth, holy and inexhaustible, is graven
> With shining furrows where his plows have gone
> Year after year, the timeless labor of stallions.
>
> The lightboned birds and beasts that cling to cover,
> The lithe fish lighting their reaches of dim water,
> All are taken, tamed in the net of his mind;
> The lion on the hill, the wild horse windy-maned,
> Resign to him; and his blunt yoke has broken
> The sultry shoulders of the mountain bull.
>
> Words also, and thought as rapid as air,
> He fashions to his good use; statecraft is his,
> And his the skill that deflects the arrows of snow,
> The spears of winter rain: from every wind
> He has made himself secure—from all but one:
> In the late wind of death he cannot stand.[39]

To only a few articulate voices in the humanistic tradition have come the power and the ability to express with wholeness and steadiness the love that bears it out, as Shakespeare once wrote, even to the edge of doom, the simultaneous comprehension of the splendor and the depravity that may be in the human spirit, and the moral realities that must enclose human existence if any stability or order can counter the vast sweep of mutability that encircles us all.

It was perhaps Shakespeare's most perceptive critic, Samuel Taylor Coleridge, who once declared that

> The truly great
> Have all one age, and from one visible space
> Shed influence! They, both in power and act,
> Are permanent, and Time is not with them,
> Save as it worketh for them, they in it.[40]

Certainly his statement is applicable to the artistic achievement and moral values that infuse *King Lear,* for the tragedy asserts and affirms a compassion not unknown to Achilles as he wept with Priam in the Grecian tents, an endurance and purification through suffering chronicled in the fortunes of Job, and a transcendence of the human spirit, through love, embodied on a mount in Galilee. The visible spaces of Shakespeare's greatest drama are part of that humanistic cosmos where indeed

> Numberless are the world's wonders, but none
> More wonderful than man.

NOTES

1. Alfred Harbage, *Shakespeare's Audience* (New York, 1961), p. 90. Other helpful sources of information about the theatrical climate of Shakespeare's day include John Cranford Adams, *The Globe Playhouse: Its Design and Equipment* (Cambridge, 1942); Joseph Quincy Adams, *Shakespearean Playhouses* (Boston, 1917); Bernard Beckerman, *Shakespeare at the Globe* (New York, 1962); Muriel St. Clare Byrne, "Shakespeare's Audience," in *Shakespeare Association, A Series of Papers on Shakespeare and the Theatre* (London, 1927), pp. 186-216; Louis B. Wright, *Middle-Class Culture in Elizabethan England* (Chapel Hill, 1935); Ashley H. Thorndike, *Shakespeare's Theater* (New York, 1916); C. Walter Hodges, *The Globe Restored* (New York, 1954); Irwin Smith, *Shakespeare's Globe Playhouse* (New York, 1956); Thomas W. Baldwin, *The Organization and Personnel of the Shakespearean Company* (Princeton, 1927); and George B. Harrison, *Elizabethan Plays and Players* (Ann Arbor, 1940). Such classic works as E. K. Chambers, *The Elizabethan Stage* (Oxford, 1923); *Henslowe's Diary* and *Henslowe's Papers*, ed. W. W. Greg (London, 1904-1908); and *Dramatic Documents from the Elizabethan Playhouses*, ed. W. W. Greg (Oxford, 1931) are essential for the advanced student. Included in the *Shakespeare Survey*, XII (1959) are a number of studies on the Elizabethan theatre.

2. The ballad is taken from *Songs from Shakespeare's Plays and Popular Songs of Shakespeare's Time*, ed. Tom Kines (New York, 1964), pp. 81-83. To determine the precise date of the ballad, as many scholars have observed, is nearly impossible. This version may or may not have antedated the play. For Shakespeare's use of song in the drama, see F. W. Sternfeld, *Music in Shakespearean Tragedy* (New York, 1963), pp. 158-194, and Peter J. Seng, *The Vocal Songs in the Plays of Shakespeare* (Cambridge, 1967) pp. 200-210.

3. *Holinshed's Chronicle as Used in Shakespeare's Plays*, ed. A. and J. Nicoll (New York, 1927); Wilfrid Perrett, "The Story of King Lear from Geoffrey of Monmouth to Shakespeare," *Paelestra*, XXXV (1904), 1-303; Irving Ribner, "Sidney's *Arcadia* and the Structure of *King Lear*," *Studia Neophilologica*, XXIV (1952), 63-68, and "Shakespeare and Legendary History," *Shakespeare Quarterly*, VII (1956), 47-52; R. H. Perkinson, "Shakespeare's Revision of the Lear Story and the Structure of *King Lear*," *Philological Quarterly*, XXII (1943), 315-329; and Robert Law, "Holinshed's Leir Story and Shakespeare's," *Studies in Philology*, XLVII (1950), 42-50.

4. William Shakespeare, *King Lear* in *Shakespeare The Complete Works*, ed. G. B. Harrison (New York, 1968), II. iv. 181-182. All subsequent references to *King Lear* are from this edition and will be indicated in parenthesis by act, scene, and line numbers within the text of this study.

The kinds of relationships with which Shakespeare is concerned in *King Lear* recall several aspects of the Aristotelian definition of tragedy: "The most important [part of tragic drama] is the structure of incidents [which form the story]. Tragedy is a representation essentially not of men but of 'human action' (*praxis*): i.e., of human life, its happiness and its misery; for on the stage these must find expression in action, and the proper end [of dramatic representation] therefore is a mode of action, not some sort of quality. . . . when the 'tragic occurrence' (*pathos*) takes place between friends—when, for instance, some such crime as murder is done or planned by brother against brother, or by son against father, or by son against mother or mother against son—here is the kind of situation that the dramatist should look for." See Aristotle, *The Poetics,* transl. and ed. Philip Wheelwright (New York, 1951), p. 297, 308.

5. Certainly the sustained focus of Andrew Cecil Bradley's *Shakespearean Tragedy* (London, 1904) concentrates on the complexity of the various Shakespearean worlds within each of the major tragedies. Samuel Taylor Coleridge's description of Hamlet's "brooding over the world within him" in *Shakespearean Criticism,* ed. Thomas Middleton Raysor (London, 1960), I, 35, perhaps establishes this critical perspective, a mode of inquiry which has led to such studies as Maynard Mack, "The World of *Hamlet*," *The Yale Review,* XLI (1952), 502-523, and Robert Heilman, "The Lear World," *English Institute Essays, 1947* (New York, 1948), pp. 29-57.

6. Aristotle, *The Poetics,* p. 317.

7. Studies on this aspect of the play are numerous. In *Shakespeare's Imagery and What It Tells Us* (Cambridge, 1966), Caroline Spurgeon observes, p. 339, that in *King Lear* "We are conscious all through of buffeting, strain, and strife, and, at moments, of bodily tension to the point of agony. So naturally does this flow from the circumstances of the drama and the mental sufferings of Lear, that we scarcely realise how greatly this sensation in us is increased by the general 'floating' image, kept constantly before us, chiefly by means of the verbs used, but also in metaphor, of a human body in anguished movement, tugged, wrenched, beaten, pierced, stung, scourged, dislocated, flayed, gashed, scalded, tortured and finally broken on the rack." See also Robert Heilman, *This Great Stage* (Baton Rouge, 1948); Wolfgang Clemen, *The Development of Shakespeare's Imagery* (Cambridge, 1951); Donald Stauffer, *Shakespeare's World of Images: The Development of His Moral Ideas* (New York, 1949); B. I. Evans, *The Language of Shakespeare's Plays* (London, 1952); G. Wilson Knight, *"King Lear* and the Comedy of the Grotesque" and "The Lear Universe" in *The Wheel of Fire* (Oxford, 1930); John Crowe Ransom, "On Shakespeare's Language," *Sewanee Review,* LV (1947), 181-198; George Kernodle, "The Symphonic Form of *King Lear"* in *Elizabethan Studies in Honor of G. F. Reynolds* (Boulder, 1945), pp. 185-191; W. R. Keast, "Imagery and Meaning of the Interpretation of *King Lear,"* *Modern Philology,* XLVII (1950), 45-64; G. W. Williams, "The Poetry of the Storm in *King Lear,"* *Shakespeare Quarterly,* II (1951), 57-71; Thelma Greenfield, "The Clothing Motif in *King Lear,"* *Shakespeare Quarterly,* V (1954), 281-286; Sigurd Burckhardt, *"King Lear:* The Quality of Nothing," *Minnesota Review,* II (1961), 33-50; Robert

Fleissner, "The 'Nothing' Element in *King Lear,*" *Shakespeare Quarterly,* XIII (1962), 67-70; John C. McCloskey, "The Emotive Use of Animal Imagery in *King Lear,*" *Shakespeare Quarterly,* XIII (1962), 321-325; Harold Skulsky, "*King Lear* and the Meaning of Chaos," *Shakespeare Quarterly,* XVII (1966), 3-17; and Paul Alpers, "*King Lear* and the Theory of the 'Sight Pattern' " in *In Defense of Reading,* ed. Reuben Brower and Richard Poirier (New York, 1963), pp. 133-152. Among the more critically provocative studies of Shakespearean artistry as a whole are Sigurd Burckhardt, *Shakespearean Meanings* (Princeton, 1968), and Norman Rabkin, *Shakespeare and the Common Understanding* (New York, 1967).

8. Willard Farnham, *The Medieval Heritage of Elizabethan Tragedy* (Oxford, 1963) remains the single best study of these patterns. See also *Lydgate's Fall of Princes,* ed. Henry Bergen (Carnegie Institution), 4 vols., Washington, 1923-1927; Lily Bess Campbell, *Tudor Conceptions of History and Tragedy in A Mirror for Magistrates* (Berkeley, 1936) and *The Mirror for Magistrates,* ed. Lily Bess Campbell (Cambridge, 1938); and C. S. Lewis, *English Literature in the Sixteenth Century* (Oxford, 1954), pp. 240-246. Other studies that deal with political theories and beliefs in Shakespearean tragedy include Paul N. Siegel, *Shakespearean Tragedy and the Elizabethan Compromise* (New York, 1957); M. M. Reese, *The Cease of Majesty* (London, 1961); L. C. Knights, "Shakespeare's Politics: With Some Reflections on the Nature of Tradition," *Proceedings of the British Academy,* XLIII (1957), 115-132; Arthur Sewell, *Character and Society in Shakespeare* (Oxford, 1951); Edwin Muir, "The Politics of *King Lear*" in *Essays on Literature and Society* (London, 1949), pp. 33-49; and W. W. Greg, "Time, Place, and Politics in *King Lear,*" *Modern Language Review,* XXXV (1940), 431-446. E. M. W. Tillyard's discussion of the nature of monarchy in *Shakespeare's History Plays* (New York, 1946) remains relevant, as does the work on Elizabethan theories of history included in Derek Traversi's *Shakespeare from Richard II to Henry V* (Stanford, 1957).

9. Thomas Norton and Thomas Sackville, *The Tragedy of [Gorboduc; Or of] Ferrex and Porrex* in *Elizabethan and Stuart Plays,* ed. Charles Read Baskerville, *et al.* (New York, 1934), I. ii. 259-261.

10. The concept is expressed most lucidly by Francis Fergusson, "The World of the Traditional Monarchy" in *Shakespeare's Tragedies of Monarchy* (New York, 1962), pp. 10-11: "The ideal order of Shakespeare's tradition, 'The Elizabethan World Picture,' as Professor Tillyard calls it, has been studied from many points of view. It is the descendant of the medieval picture, in which Greek notions of the order of nature and the stars were combined with the cosmic drama of man's fall and redemption, as embodied in the Christian creed. Human society, when obedient to faith and reason, was supposed to reflect, in a small figure, God's cosmic order. The symbolic figure of the king was at the center. The man who occupied that awesome position was supposed to try to harmonize in his own life, and in his rule, the life of his people in its time with the eternal and unseen truth of God. . . . Shakespeare's audience . . . believed that the monarch was the foundation of their security, the guarantor of the ancient tradition that was embodied in the laws, institutions, customs, and ceremonies, both religious

and secular, of their society. . . . In each play the nature of the man who is king defines, within the traditional framework, the moral world of that tragedy." See also Theodore Spencer, *Shakespeare and the Nature of Man* (New York, 1942) and E. M. W. Tillyard, *The Elizabethan World Picture* (London, 1943). A significant study of this philosophical concept also appears in Ernst Cassirer, *The Individual and the Cosmos in Renaissance Philosophy*, transl. Mario Domandi (New York, 1963).

Among works which treat Shakespeare's exploration of the meaning of nature in *King Lear*, see H. B. Charlton, *Shakespearian Tragedy* (Cambridge, 1952); John Danby, *Shakespeare's Doctrine of Nature: A Study of King Lear* (London, 1949); Geoffrey Bush, *Shakespeare and the Natural Condition* (Cambridge, 1956); and Robert Speaight, *Nature in Shakespearian Tragedy* (New York, 1962).

11. Cf. the comments of the major Romantic Shakespearean critics. Coleridge, *Criticism,* I, 49: "Of all Shakespeare's plays Macbeth is the most rapid, Hamlet the slowest, in movement. Lear combines length with rapidity,—like the hurricane and the whirlpool, absorbing while it advances." Charles Lamb once noted: "The greatness of Lear is not in corporal dimensions, but in intellectual: the explosions of his passion are terrible as a volcano; they are storms turning up and disclosing to the bottom that sea, his mind, with all its vast riches. It is his mind which is laid bare." See *The Complete Works and Letters of Charles Lamb* (New York, 1935), p. 298. A similar metaphorical context infuses the statement of William Hazlitt: "The mind of Lear, staggering between the weight of attachment and the hurried movements of passion, is like a tall ship driven about by the winds, buffeted by the furious waves, but that still rides above the storm, having its anchor fixed in the bottom of the sea." See *The Round Table and Characters of Shakespear's Plays* (London, 1944), p. 258. See also G. Wilson Knight, *The Shakespearian Tempest* (London, 1953) for an extensive discussion of the sea patterns in Shakespearean comedy and tragedy.

12. Coleridge, *Criticism,* I, 59: "Surely, never was such a scene conceived before or since. Take it but as a picture for the eye only, it is more terrific than any a Michael Angelo [*sic*] inspired by a Dante could have conceived, and which none but a Michael Angelo could have executed. Or let it have been uttered to the blind, the howlings of convulsed nature would seem converted into the voice of conscious humanity."

13. Theodore Spencer, *Shakespeare and the Nature of Man*, p. 137: "The main action is also re-inforced in this play by more characters than in any other who act as a chorus. . . . in addition to such minor figures as Curan, two or three Gentlemen and Cornwall's servants, we have Kent, the Fool, Edgar and Albany—all of whom, in various ways, comment on the action and both re-inforce and expand its implications. Even Lear himself in his madness—and at this point Shakespeare uses to the fullest possible extent the resources of the Elizabethan stage convention of presenting mad scenes— even Lear himself acts as a chorus to his own situation, and in the fourth act, his madness giving him an extra personality, he comments with desperate irony on the general evil and injustice which for the moment are more universal than the particular evil and injustice that have driven him insane."

34

14. For studies on the significance of the allusions to Fortune in *King Lear* and in regard to emblem and iconography in Renaissance drama in general, see Farnham, *Medieval Heritage;* Russell Fraser, *Shakespeare's Poetics in Relation to King Lear* (London, 1962); Samuel Claggett Chew, *The Pilgrimage of Life* (New Haven, 1962); Henry Green, *Shakespeare and the Emblem Writers* (London, 1870. Reprinted, New York, 1966); and Howard Patch, *The Goddess Fortuna in Medieval Literature* (New York, 1967). Bernard Spivack in *Shakespeare and the Allegory of Evil* (New York, 1958) and William Elton, *King Lear and the Gods* (San Marino, 1966) also provide much helpful information.

15. Fergusson, "Introduction to *King Lear,*" *Monarchy,* p. 268.

16. *Shakespeare and the Nature of Man,* pp. 136-137. See also George Kernodle, "Symphonic Form," p. 186: *"King Lear* is built on this same artistic principle of correspondence or parallelism. Each motif is repeated in as many ways as possible. Each character repeats or balances some other character; each event is the prefiguration of some other event; and structural units are balanced against each other. Further, each theme is repeated in the wit and imagery. Just as the main theme of the violation of natural law is explored in three domains—the individual character, the social state, and the wider universe of stars and tempests—so the artistic method may be traced in its three domains—the alignment of characters, the structure of scenes, and the verbal imagery." See also Edward Block, *"King Lear:* A Study in Balanced and Shifting Sympathies," *Shakespeare Quarterly,* X (1959), 499-512.

17. Winifred Nowottny, "Lear's Questions," *Shakespeare Survey,* X (1957), 90-97, discusses briefly some of the major questions posed in the drama and suggests that "The whole play is a dramatic answer to the one question in which all Lear's questions are subsumed: the question, What is man?" Any study of question in the drama involves technicalities of punctuation in the Elizabethan-Jacobean era. Many scholars have noted that the question mark and exclamation point were used interchangeably by Tudor-Stuart printers. See Percy Simpson, *Shakespearian Punctuation* (Oxford, 1911), p. 8, pp. 85-86.

Heilman, *Stage,* is perhaps the fullest study of major patterns of paradox. See also Sholom Kahn, " 'Enter Lear mad,' " *Shakespeare Quarterly,* VIII (1957), 311-329; Carolyn French, "Shakespeare's 'Folly': *King Lear,*" *Shakespeare Quarterly,* X (1959), 523-529; Robert Goldsmith, *Wise Fools in Shakespeare* (East Lansing, 1955); Enid Welsford, *The Fool* (New York, 1935); William Empson, "Fool in *Lear,*" *Sewanee Review,* LVII (1949), 177-214; and Jonas Barish and Marshall Waingrow, " 'Service' in *King Lear,*" *Shakespeare Quarterly,* IX (1958), 347-355.

18. Maynard Mack, *King Lear in Our Time* (Berkeley, 1965), p. 117, comments: "Tragedy never tells us what to think; it shows us what we are and may be. And what we are and may be was never, I submit, more memorably fixed upon a stage than in this kneeling old man whose heartbreak is precisely the measure of what, in our world of relatedness, it is possible to lose and possible to win. The victory and the defeat are simultaneous and inseparable. . . . *King Lear* . . . begs us to seek the meaning of our human fate not in what becomes of us, but in what we become.

Death, as we saw, is miscellaneous and commonplace; it is life whose quality may be made noble and distinctive. Suffering we all recoil from; but we know it is a greater thing to suffer than to lack the feelings and virtues that make it possible to suffer. Cordelia, we may choose to say, accomplished nothing, yet we know it is better to have been Cordelia than to have been her sisters. When we come crying hither, we bring with us the badge of all our misery; but it is also the badge of the vulnerabilities that give us access to whatever grandeur we achieve."

19. A. C. Bradley's discussion of this aspect of the play in *Shakespearean Tragedy* remains apt as do the views of Thedore Spencer, *Shakespeare and the Nature of Man*, pp. 149-150, and Richard Sewall, *The Vision of Tragedy* (New Haven, 1962), pp. 4-5: "The tragic vision is in its first phase primal, or primitive, in that it calls up out of the depths the first (and last) of all questions, the question of existence: What does it mean to be? It recalls the original terror, harking back to a world that antedates the conceptions of philosophy, the consolations of the later religions, and whatever constructions the human mind has devised to persuade itself that its universe is secure. It recalls the original unreason, the terror of the irrational. It sees man as questioner, naked, unaccommodated, alone, facing mysterious, demonic forces in his own nature and outside, and the irreducible facts of suffering and death. . . . Here, with all the protective covering stripped off, the hero faces as if no man had ever faced it before the existential question—Job's question, 'What is man?' or Lear's, 'Is man no more than this?' " A major discussion of Lear and the storm scene remains Derek Traversi, *"King Lear," Scrutiny*, XIX (1953), 43-64, 126-142, 206-230. See also Catherine Dunn, "The Storm in *King Lear," Shakespeare Quarterly*, III (1952), 329-333; Josephine Waters Bennett, "The Storm Within: The Madness of Lear," *Shakespeare Quarterly*, XIII (1962), 137-155; Williams, "Poetry of the Storm"; Kernodle, "Symphonic Form"; and Skulsky, "Chaos."

20. For a particularly lucid commentary on the self-knowledge motif of the tragedy, see Paul Jorgensen, *Lear's Self-Discovery* (Berkeley, 1967), as well as Robert Heilman, " 'Twere Best Not Know Myself': Othello, Lear, Macbeth," *Shakespeare Quarterly*, XV (1964), 89-98; and Northrop Frye, *Fools of Time* (Toronto, 1967), pp. 103ff. Intertwined with Lear's search for knowledge of self is his exploration of justice. Among numerous studies of this concept are Irving Ribner, "The Gods Are Just: A Reading of *King Lear," Tulane Drama Review*, II (1958), 34-54; Dorothy Hockey, "The Trial Pattern in *King Lear," Shakespeare Quarterly*, X (1959), 389-395; and J. L. Rosier, "The *Lex Aeterna* and *King Lear," Journal of English and Germanic Philology*, LIII (1954), 574-580.

Among many studies which discuss major thematic concerns, see Derek Traversi, *An Approach to Shakespeare* (New York, 1956); Harold Wilson, *On the Design of Shakespearian Tragedy* (Toronto, 1957); L. C. Knights, *Some Shakespearean Themes* (Stanford, 1960); and Irving Ribner, *Patterns in Shakespearean Tragedy* (London, 1960). See also D. G. James, *The Dream of Learning* (Oxford, 1951) for a commentary on the kinds of knowledge with which the tragedy deals, as well as J. V. Cunningham, *Woe or Wonder: The Emotional Effects of Shakespearean Tragedy* (Boulder, 1951) and J. M. Lothian, *King Lear: A Tragic Reading of Life* (London, 1950).

21. Cf. Douglas Bush, *The Renaissance and English Humanism* (Toronto, 1939), p. 96: "It is that simultaneous double vision of man which gives the literature of the English Renaissance its ethical strength and centrality, its heights and depths of tragic emotion."

22. That Lear is restored to a kingdom of reason, wisdom, and love—a realm more important than a physical country—is a commonplace in much Shakespearean criticism. The Shakespearean conception of both the temporal and the eternal is nowhere better dramatized than in this scene, so soon to be followed by the catastrophe of the conclusion. In "The World of the Traditional Monarchy," p. 13, Francis Fergusson notes this quality of fused particularity and broad expansiveness within the drama: "Shakespeare's sense of the temporal dimension of the human situation accounts for the extraordinarily concrete reality of his human scenes. It enabled him to see evil in all the contingencies of time and place, but at the same time it also enabled him to qualify the pessimism of that vision. History, governed by an unfathomable fate or providence, is partly to blame, and when the dark time is passed we can glimpse against the possibility of the true order. The ends of these tragedies bring not only terror and mourning, but also reaffirmation and reconciliation." See also Spencer, *Shakespeare and the Nature of Man*, pp. 150-152, for a further discussion of Lear's "recovery into love," and G. L. Bickersteth, "The Golden World of *King Lear,*" *Proceedings of the British Academy*, XXXII (1947), 147-171. Other commentaries on these basic operative values within the tragedy include Sears Jayne, "Charity in *King Lear,*" *Shakespeare Quarterly*, XV (1964), 277-288 and Paul Siegel, "Adversity and the Miracle of Love in *King Lear,*" *Shakespeare Quarterly*, VI (1955), 325-336. In *Shakespeare: His Mind and His Art* (London, 1898), Edward Dowden noted, p. 239, that within the ethical framework of Stoicism of the play "the presence of human virtue, fidelity, and self-sacrificial love" was a dominant force. A study of Platonic and Aristotelian ethical aspects of the drama is Hardin Craig, "The Ethics of *King Lear,*" *Philological Quarterly*, IV (1925), 97-109.

23. V. iii. 170-171: "The gods are just, and of our pleasant vices/Make instruments to plague us." I have avoided extensive discussion of the critical controversy that exists about the ending of the tragedy. In this study I use the terms redemptive and sacrificial in essentially a humanistic sense, not in any attempt to establish Christian analogues or draw upon Christian tradition. I suggest that the love which redeems nature from the general curse may be considered in the human contexts of commitment, dedication, and preservation of bond. One of the better surveys of criticism on this particular problem occurs in Elton, *Gods*, pp. 3-8, where the well-known views of A. C. Bradley, R. W. Chambers, G. Wilson Knight, J. Dover Wilson, J. Lothian, and P. Siegel are contrasted to the more pessimistic readings of E. K. Chambers, Clifford Leech, F. P. Wilson, G. B. Harrison, Arthur Sewell, D. G. James, and A. H. R. Fairchild. Certainly the Christian redemptionist theory of Roy Battenhouse, "Shakespearean Tragedy: A Christian Interpretation" in *The Tragic Vision and the Christian Faith*, ed. Nathan Scott (New York, 1957), pp. 56-98; and *Shakespearean Tragedy: Its Art and Its Christian Premises* (Bloomington, 1969), or Oscar J. Campbell,

Designed and prepared by the Publications Office, Ball State University